HIBBERT LECTURES

LIBERALITY AND CIVILIZATION

AMS PRESS
NEW YORK

LIBERALITY AND CIVILIZATION

Lectures given at the invitation of the Hibbert Trustees
in the Universities of Bristol, Glasgow, and
Birmingham in October and
November 1937

by

GILBERT MURRAY

D.C.L., LL.D., LITT.D.

LONDON
GEORGE ALLEN & UNWIN LTD
MUSEUM STREET

Library of Congress Cataloging in Publication Data

Murray, Gilbert, 1866–1957.
  Liberality and civilization.

  Reprint of the 1938 ed. published by G. Allen &
Unwin, London, which was issued in the 1937
Hibbert lectures series.
  1. Liberalism—Addresses, essays, lectures.
2. World politics—Addresses, essays, lectures.
3. Civilization—Addresses, essays, lectures.
I. Title.   II. Series: Hibbert lectures
(London); 1937.
HM278.M87   1980   320.5'1   77-27139
ISBN 0-404-60430-7

This edition is reprinted by arrangement with
Macmillan Publishing Co., Inc.

Reprinted from the edition of 1938, London. Trim size of the original has been slightly altered. [original trim size: 10.6 × 18 cm]. Text area of the original remains the same.

No State or policy can prosper unless the ground-
work is moral. The ethical basis of all politics
is humanity, and humanity is an international
programme. It is a new word for the old love of
our fellow-men.

No State can be managed without recognition
of the ethical basis of politics, and no State can
long stand if it infringes the broad rules of human
morality. The Greeks and Romans declared justice to be the foundation of states; and justice is
the arithmetic of love.

President Masaryk

Introductory Note

If the censures passed in these lectures strike more at some countries than others, it is not because of any prejudice in my mind against those countries. I have many friends in all of them, and owe a large debt of gratitude and admiration to the literature and art of all. It is only War and the war mentality that I regard as an enemy; only those Governments who plot aggression against their neighbours that make collaboration and friendly settlement impossible.

G. M.

*Liberality and
Civilization*

I

I

I WAS LATELY at an international gathering where, in the course of conversation, one of the most distinguished historians in Europe made a remark which set us all thinking. "In my country," he said, "practically everyone wants a Liberal policy; in economics, in education, in international relations, in everything. If Europe as a whole does not adopt Liberal policies we feel that it may be the end of civilization. Yet the Liberal party is nearly dead, and no Liberal has much chance of getting elected to parliament." I ventured to observe that things were not very different in England; and several other speakers, from one nationality after another, joined in, saying it was much the same in their own countries. I was reminded of a conversation I had with a Balkan statesman just after the war. He had been talking to the late Mr. Headlam-Morley of the Foreign Office, and said to me: "Yes, that is English Liberalism. If we had three statesmen like that in the Balkans we should have peace." As a matter of fact Headlam-Morley called himself a Conservative, but by Balkan standards he was a most enlightened Liberal.

Now what is this thing that most of Europe longs for, this thing for the lack of which European civilization is perhaps on the verge of perishing, but which nevertheless no country seems able to achieve or even dares to profess? That is the subject that I propose to discuss in these two lectures. I call it "Liberality," not "Liberalism," partly because I wish to keep clear of mere party politics. My main wish is that whatever party any one of you belongs to, he may bring more Liberality into it. Partly because I remember John Morley once telling me how Mr. Gladstone used to ask about people who, as far as votes went, were his undoubted followers, "Is he a man of real Liberality?" Real Liberality, wherever it may be found, is the subject that I want to study.

I know that the appeal I wish to make to you is out of fashion. That is why I make it. And I would ask you not to assume that when I say Liberality I really mean something else. I do not mean Left as against Right; both these terms are too vague, and tyranny remains tyranny whether practised by Mussolini or by Stalin. I do not mean Democracy as opposed to Oligarchy or Aristocracy. Democracies can be violently anti-Liberal, as they were in England and France and America at the end of the war, as "Tory Democracy" definitely claims to be. Often enough in history Liberality has been defended by an unpopular few. I do not mean individualism as against socialism; very much the reverse except in one respect. Liberality must necessarily be concerned with the common good; it is only individualist in the sense of insisting that, in the last resort, each man must maintain his personal freedom, must obey his own conscience and not be content to be merely an item in a multitude Nor do I wish to associate the word Liberal too closely with the desire for one's own liberty. I see that Signor Mussolini complains that the League of Nations interferes with his liberty; that does not make him a Liberal. The man who said "Give me Liberty or give me death" was himself a slave-owner. One cannot call that "real Liberality." I do not even mean a desire for general unrestricted personal liberty of action as opposed to authority. In some modern societies personal licence has at times reached a point where it is dangerous to the common weal. Law is the condition of freedom; the individuals or classes which are left undisciplined either by their own ideals or by public opinion are almost certain to come into conflict with some harsher compulsion.

As a political term the word "liberal" was, curiously enough, taken from Spain in the early nineteenth century. It denoted there, in a land of great social oppression, of narrow and ignorant prejudice both religious and monarchical, a movement for a more generous outlook, a breaking of chains, an opposition to the Church and the monarchy, and a sympathy with the oppressed. It had, if I read the movement at all rightly, a strong element of that chivalry and sense of honour which has been always as characteristic of Spain as its contrary outburts of intolerance and cruelty. But, leaving Spain and the fortunes of Spanish liberalism aside, the derivation of the word "Liberal" is plain enough: "Liber" is a free man, and the adjective "liberalis" means "like a free man," or "having the quality of a free man." It is a Roman idea derived from the Greek; and here I must ask you to excuse an old Greek professor, who can never quite escape from the spell of those great teachers and writers who have been his life's companions. In the ancient world, where slavery was a common fact and a constant problem to the human conscience, philosophers were fond of pointing out how few men were really free. Is a drunkard or an opium addict free? Can he exercise his will? Is he not the slave of his own craving? Men are constantly the slaves of their passions, of their prejudices, above all of their fears: they cannot think, they cannot choose their line of action, they are as much slaves as the gangs who work under the overseer's lash.

Some of these slaveries are internal, some purely external. Man in a pre-civilized state, if we indulge our imaginations in trying to conceive a condition of which we have no historical record, cannot attain much freedom. His life is not merely, in Hobbes' picturesque phrase, "solitary, poor, nasty, brutish, and short." He is, like my fellow-countrymen the Australian aborigines, a prey to hunger and thirst, a prey to heat and cold, a prey to wild beasts better armed than himself, or to human enemies more formidable still. His necessities drive him. He must have food and drink; he must have shelter, he must have some protection, or else he dies. And the first thing that civilization does is to provide for these elementary needs of man and thus make him to that extent free. In Greek thought the first great necessity of civilization is a *Polis*, a word which we translate "City" but which seems strictly speaking to have meant a circuit wall. Inside the wall men could rest and breathe freely; they were no longer in constant fear, like terrified beasts. And inside the wall they had the other great primal necessity, fire, a common fire which all were bound to worship and which must never be allowed to die. Through that fire and that wall a man became a member of a society, bound to co-operate with others as they with him, a society based on mutual help day by day, mutual protection in case of danger, and the observance of common laws or customs. This implies an enormous release from fear, an insurance not merely against violent death, robbery, and persecution from outside enemies, but against most of the elementary cruelties and injustices of internal anarchy. The city was built, as Aristotle says, that man might live; it continues that he may "live well." And to "live well" in Aristotle's sense, means to develop all the complicated arts and laws, moral, social, and economic, which go to the making of a good and progressive society. The city gave man that great necessity of civilization without which freedom soon perishes, a superfluity or reserve. A reserve of wealth, whereby to keep oneself alive through special trials and have something to give to others who need it more. A reserve of security, whereby, not being always on the edge of fear, man can afford to be tolerant, to be kindly, to listen to opinions or put up with habits which differ from his own. A reserve of leisure, from which proceeds all progress, all increase of knowledge and reflection, all the sciences and arts. It is worth while remembering that our word "school" is simply a transliteration of the Greek word for "leisure" (σχολή). The Roman equivalent was *ludus*, "play."

So far, I think, most people will agree. The

next characteristic of Liberality is one of fundamental importance. A free man must obviously
be able to think freely. If he is deliberately har-
nessed in blinkers or forced into a particular
groove from which he cannot escape, he is not
like a free man, not "liberalis." And in order to
think freely he must have freedom of speech. It
is not merely that most of our serious and useful
thinking is the result of talking things over with
other people: the thoughts of a man who never
expresses himself and never listens to other men
cannot remain healthy or normal. But beyond
that it is for most people quite impossible to think
clearly without putting the thought into words,
looking at it and trying again. To deny the right
of free speech results in a denial of free thought;
and to be denied the power of thinking is the
direst slavery.

The limitations that have to be imposed, or at
any rate are imposed, on free speech and thought
in various societies are usually in exact propor-
tion to the degree in which that society has lost
its reserve of security and thus fallen away from
civilization. The more truly a society is civilized
the more fully speech and thought within its pre-
cincts are free. Uniformity of thought is no doubt
useful for war and for aggressive campaigns of
propaganda; but for the people of a civilized and
peaceful community variety is far more valuable.

Only through variety, through discussion, experiment, contradiction, and correction is there much prospect of thinking better and more clearly, so as to progress towards the understanding of justice or truth. Hence we find almost always in Liberality another quality, later and rarer in its growth, a spirit of scepticism. This is a natural result of enlightenment. The anthropologists have shown us how in every normal human group, from highest to lowest, "Custom is King." Take any society you like in history. You will find in it a great cloudy mass of accepted traditional beliefs, habits, prejudices, and superstitions which we now know to have been mistaken. Always you will find the great mass of people believing, the popularity hunters pretending to believe, and the liberals questioning, those accepted traditions. The Liberal will constantly be appealing to the authorities and the multitude of his nation as Oliver Cromwell to his Council: "I beseech you by the bowels of Christ to remember that it is possible you may be mistaken." That does not mean that we ought to have no ardent faith or strong convictions. Very much the reverse. Our convictions must stand criticism. Where conviction degenerates into fanaticism and becomes really harmful is, I think, almost always in cases where the intellectual belief is surrounded and swamped by a mass of passions which are supposed to be dependent upon it but are really sprung from quite other sources. A man may have intense beliefs about the Filioque clause or the miracle-working powers of Lenin's portrait: no one can be quite certain he is wrong. But as soon as he begins to hate and persecute those who do not hold the same beliefs we can definitely blame him. He is doing wrong to his fellow creatures, and the pretext with which he excuses himself is false. Any careful analysis of his motives will almost certainly show that his fury is not really due to the speculative difference but to some form of partisan passion, mainly no doubt to the fear that if the heretics get into power he and his friends will lose their positions and perhaps be the victims of a pogrom. A Byzantine political mob once carried the head of an adherent of the opposite party on a pike labelled ''This is the head of the friend of the enemy of the Holy Trinity.'' A famous Rumanian anti-semite has recently explained that as a good Christian he could forgive many wrongs, ''but the blood of the Son of God he could never forgive.'' An existing Catholic catechism in Spain contains the question, ''What kind of sin is committed by those who vote Liberal?'' and the answer, ''Mortal sin.'' I greatly doubt whether in any of these cases the alleged religious motive counted for much, or indeed anything. Fear, greed, envy, political passion, and perhaps the mere spirit of revenge which arises in all protracted conflicts, had ever so much more influence. I think, then, that a good Liberal should be sceptical in two senses: first, if he realizes the constant advance of knowledge and the consequent correction by each subsequent age of the beliefs firmly held by the last, he will bear in mind Cromwell's counsel and know that, hard as we ought to struggle to attain truth, we shall never have attained it in full; secondly, that however sure he may be about some particular speculative belief he should remember that it covers only a small part of the world, and that people may be wrong about that part and yet triumphantly right and worthy of respect about a thousand others. We have got beyond the point where to be a bloody Protestant, or a blinded Papist, or a follower of the ''false Mahound,'' was necessarily to be a villain. We have now to remember to feel the same tolerance towards Capitalist and Proletarian, Fascist and Communist. Religions, institutions, customs, differ so widely from region to region that we tend to forget that one of the most certain things in the world is the moral law. Justice, good faith, kindness, temperance, courage are things recognized and admired in the earliest ages of man as well as the latest, by the natives of Central

Australia or West Africa as much as by those of London or Paris. A Liberal should always make sure that no speculative belief makes him break that law. Against injustice, falsehood, bad faith, cruelty, and the denial of the human conscience, Liberality stands unshakably firm: for there the centre of its religion is touched.

These, then, I suggest, are the characteristics of true civilization. It sets man free; free from the pressure of daily fear inasmuch as it provides Security; free from the pressure of daily hunger and thirst as it provides a reserve of wealth; free to do the things he really wants to do instead of merely what he must do in order to keep alive, free to make poetry and music, to pursue art and science, to think and speak and create. Civilization is not a purely material thing, though it has in it a large material element, and a civilization that goes wrong, like a religion that goes wrong, may well do more harm than good. Edward Carpenter makes a plausible case against most modern societies in his little book, *Civilization, its Cause and Cure*. Tolstoy, while we are under the spell of his enchanting sophistries, makes us feel that an ignorant, superstitious, hard-working Russian moujik is a happier and better being than any of our great statesmen or artists or men of science. None the less, if we have any faith in the meaning of life and the process of history, if we believe that there is any value in human effort, we are bound, I think, to believe that it is a great and precious achievement that Raphael should have painted his Madonnas, that Newton should have discovered the Law of Gravitation and Einstein calculated the movement of light, that Aeschylus and Shakespeare should have written their great tragedies; that it is, so to speak, upon these paths that man must advance if he is to fulfill some great purpose like that described in theological language in the old Scottish catechism, "to glorify God and enjoy him for ever."

Here, then, is the answer to the puzzle from which we started. We have lost Liberality in Europe because we have so largely lost the main elements of civilization, and conversely we have lost these because we have so failed in liberality. We have lost security. The three great militarist Powers have formally rejected the civilized ideals of law and liberality and announced a policy of lawless predatory ambition. They all proclaim the glory and necessity of war, and give practical emphasis to their doctrines by an intense and systematic militarization of the whole social structure and day-to-day habits of their peoples. This destroys security between nation and nation; while the Russian revolution with its powerful reverberations abroad threatens security between class and class.* In all the states I have mentioned internal security and confidence in the law have diminished or vanished, and innocence is no protection against imprisonment, torture, or death. Many nations have lost their reserve of distributed wealth. There are some million of ruined and beggared refugees from the four countries named, most of them quite innocent of crime and most of them still without settled shelter. In most countries among manual workers and brain-workers alike there is poverty and unemployment to-day and fear of worse to-morrow. The

* Cf. General Kork: "Imperialist war represents the surest means of achieving the Revolution and the setting up of the Soviet regime throughout the world. The Red Army will then be thrown into the scales to hasten on the Revolution. If the masses of Western Europe are unwilling by themselves to ensure the dictatorship of the proletariat, then the Red Army will, if need be by force, step into the breach." This is the old Trotskyist doctrine of world-revolution, now condemned by Stalin. General Kork has been executed. One must compare Mussolini's message to the Italian troops defeated in Spain that their mission was "To impose fascism on Spain by war." Also his speech on October 27, 1930: "The struggle develops from now onward over a world-wide area. . . . Fascism is on the agenda in all countries, feared in this country, hated implacably in that, and elsewhere invoked with ardour. The phrase 'Fascism is not an article for export' is not mine. To-day I affirm that Fascism as an idea, a doctrine, a realization, is universal." Quoted by Commander King-Hall in *The Times*, September 1937.

world has lost leisure, at least that fruitful and untroubled leisure from which spring the great advances of human thought; and in the totalitarian countries thought itself, whether in science, art, or religion, is deliberately persecuted. No wonder that in such a world, surrounded on every side by threats of violence, Governments do not dare to be Liberal. Each class, each nation is tempted selfishly to concentrate upon its own safety and to fight for its own hand.

Conversely it is easy enough to see that this loss of civilization is caused by a failure of Liberality. The Great War in the first place; for war is the extreme denial of liberality, and, except in its own technical sphere, of civilization. It has left behind it a legacy of illiberality and barbarism. An illiberal international policy towards the beaten nations; an illiberal trade policy, checking and distorting the whole commerce and industry of the world; and often an illiberal home policy, turning what ought to be a discussion of principles and measures for the good of the community into an economic struggle between classes.

I will not pursue this analysis farther. I assume that few of us here wish to acquiesce in this deterioration of human life; but what are we to do? What do I mean when I say that Liberality is what is needed to stop the deterioration and restore to the world its lost civilization, its lost freedom? In the first place, I repeat, I am no talking party politics. Secondly, I do not mean that what is wanted is merely a middle policy between Left and Right; still less a middle-class policy avoiding the other class policies of capital and labour respectively. In only one sense do I want a middle-class policy. I see that Herr Hitler in *Mein Kampf* (p. 475) exalts the value of ''fanatical, yea, hysterical passion'' against what he calls the ''bourgeois virtues of peace and order''; on that issue I am all for the bourgeois. But by Liberality, both in private life and public policy, I mean something different.

First of all, I accept the reproach that all through the ancient world, the *liberi*, the ἐλεύθεροι, were a privileged class, lifted above a vast unprivileged mass who were not free. In the full sense of the word ''free'' the same is true of the modern world also. Well, I ask you to be and feel yourselves to be in the midst of this demoralized world a privileged class. Seize the privilege of being free seekers after truth, champions of the oppressed, indifferent to mere orthodoxy and popularity. It is only a limited number of persons who have the material freedom which comes from a reserve of wealth, leisure, and security; a still more limited number have the moral and internal freedom from prejudice, fear, self-seeking, and the like, which is required to make a man genuinely "Liberalis." True enough. It is a great privilege to be Liberal, though it is not a privilege mainly dependent on wealth. Here again my ancient philosophers have something to say. They are never tired of telling us that the way to be rich is not to acquire large sums of money; it is to be master of your wants and desires, to be content with what you have and able to help others. To be rich depends on that internal feeling of having enough to give something away: enough security to be able to comfort those who are afraid, enough leisure to give some thought to those who need thinking for, as well as enough money or food or shelter to be able to share it with a friend. Trade Unionists are not, in the ordinary sense, grossly affluent persons. But they contrived, I see, to send £68,000 to the distressed working people of Vienna. I regard the people who were able and willing to do that as a highly privileged class. As a matter of fact, no doubt, English Liberals have generally been in the ordinary sense a privileged class, but always a privileged class which wished to give, not to take, to help, not to claim help, to extend its own privileges to wider and wider circles. If you take the history of the Liberal movements in Europe during the nineteenth

century you will find consistently the same process: members of a privileged class working to
have their privileges extended to others. It was
people who had the vote who worked to have
the franchise given to the voteless; Christians
who worked for the emancipation of Jews, Pro-
testants for the emancipation of Catholics, members of the Church of England who abolished the
Test Acts. The same with the legalization of the
Trade Union, the abolition of slavery, the protection of native races: always a privileged class
working for the extension of their privilege, or
sometimes for its transformation from a privilege
into a common right of humanity. Those whole
campaigns were essentially liberal campaigns. To
work for them implied a conquest over self-
interest, the interest of the privileged in maintaining their privileges. It implied a conquest
over fear: fear that the Jews, the Catholics, the
Nonconformists, the working classes in general,
could not be trusted and, because they felt
bitterly against governments which treated them
unjustly, might prove enemies of the State when
their treatment was just. It implied clearly a conquest over mere prejudice, the prejudice of
people accustomed to a social system and a way
of thinking which they had not the mental energy
to criticize. The reforms could not be carried
except by a great effort of liberality: an effort by

which men made themselves free of self-interest, free of fear, free of prejudice, and were able to see facts and judge policies as free men should.

Of course human motives are always mixed, and those of politicians more mixed than most, but there is one current conception of the Liberal movement of the nineteenth century that seems to me completely untrue: the idea that it was merely a middle-class movement devoted to the interests of the middle classes. Such an idea could never have arisen except through the influence of what is perhaps the greatest and the most infectious of all the fallacies of Karl Marx, the theory that all human action, or at any rate all collective action, is based on the pursuit of direct material interest. It is an idea which, like many others widely current at the present day, owes its success not to its truth, nor even to its appearance of truth when exposed to criticism, but to two particular plausibilities. In the first place it fulfills a wish, in the second it is supported by crowds and crowds of instances in ordinary life. I should compare it with Christian Science or with Anti-Semitism. Christian Science tells us that all illness is imaginary and unreal. Well, we should love to think so, and we all of us have met with people who spend their time worrying over their various complaints, but recover rapidly if they get busy about something else and cease to think of themselves. So much of human illness is unreal that, by a pleasing jump, one can maintain that it is all unreal. The same with Anti-Semitism; attribute all human ills to the greed and sensuality of the Jews, and, since those faults are common to most of humanity, you will find hundreds of Jews who are good instances of your theory. Similarly, all history and all contemporary social life teems with instances of persons and classes who are influenced, in whole or in part, openly or secretly, by the desire for their own material advantage. In ordinary commercial dealings this is admitted; a man seeks a higher salary or a higher price for his goods without further excuse. But, Marx points out, in social and political matters, when a man wants something that is to his own advantage but cannot get it unless other people are persuaded to agree with him, he naturally has to find some other considerations which are likely to move them. He tries to persuade them—and constantly succeeds in persuading himself—that the action which happens to increase his profit is only desired by him because it is just, because it is moral or religious, because it is for the good of the country. No doubt this dash of humbug occurs extremely often; and it is easy enough to make the jump and say that it occurs always; that people are always actuated by their material economic advantage and that, when they put forward any other motive, they are lying. Such a doctrine is of enormous convenience to a certain type of political agitator. Yet it is obviously untrue. Karl Marx himself showed remarkable indifference to his own economic interest when he lived for years in great poverty writing an immense book for which no publisher was likely to pay him. Study his life and you can see that he was moved by all sorts of motives, by vanity, by ambition, by jealousy and ill temper, by intellectual interest, and by a magnificent unselfish idealism. Economic considerations were seldom present to Marx, except when the pinch of poverty became really painful and in 'a burst of irritation he insisted, unreasonably enough, that someone else should pay for him. Think of any of the great individuals who have moved mankind during the last century: Darwin, Wilberforce, John Stuart Mill, Einstein; no doubt you will find in them here and there beliefs or ways of thought due to their class or nationality or to mere tradition, but in their main activities you will find scarcely a trace of the economic motive. Think of the people we know personally; do we not know many who are guided, when occasion arises, to say nothing of worse motives, by a disinterested hatred of injustice and cruelty, by religious or non-religious idealism, or by mere good will and humanity? And if we turn from individuals to communities, and consider the national passions which are devastating the present world, is it not mere wilful blindness to ignore the motives of revenge, inherited prejudice, national ambition, and vanity; to suppose that it is an economic motive which makes Germans prefer guns to butter, or Arabs to hate the Jews whose presence in Palestine has increased their wages and improved the value of their estates? I dwell at some length on the falseness of this delusive Marxian prejudice, not merely because I think it is as a matter of fact untrue, but because if accepted and really believed it would undermine our whole faith in ethical values and the possibility of justice and charity between man and man.

I should be more inclined to think that, as a matter of psychology, we overrate the element of pure material selfishness in determining public policy. All sorts of sentimental elements play their part. The defence of various iniquities gets entangled with the love of home, of parents, of friends, with the idealized memories of one's own youth and of old familiar beloved things. For example, if you consider the England of the early nineteenth century, and the appalling abuses with which it was penetrated through and through, the savage criminal law, the press-gang, the open sale of commissions in the army, the rotten boroughs, the merciless floggings and executions, the almost universal corruption and drunkenness of the ruling classes, it gives you a shock to find a kindly and imaginative man of genius like Scott, or even a reformer like Canning, defending them; to find so shrewd a man as the Duke of Wellington saying, with obvious sincerity, when defending the system of rotten boroughs, that it seemed to him to surpass the limits of human wisdom—"indeed, I should almost call it an emanation of a higher mind." He was certainly not thinking of his economic interest, perhaps not even really thinking very exclusively of the rotten boroughs; he was thinking of the days and scenes, the memories, the persons, that he loved in England, all that he had fought for and striven for throughout his life, and then transferring his emotion to something quite different: the constitution of English society. He felt perhaps towards England rather as Lord Baldwin does. It hurt him to think of altering a thing so beautiful.

That explanation may perhaps help us to understand something that at first sight seems unreasonable in Conservatism. As for Liberalism, those who have never taken part in its great campaigns—and I fear that phrase now comprises the great majority—have a difficulty in understanding what Liberality means, or what it was that kindled their fathers and grandfathers to such a fire of enthusiasm. I shall have more to say about this in my second lecture, but for the moment I would point out that this difficulty of understanding is partly due to historical causes. Battles once won lose their interest: the result is accepted as a matter of course and the long struggle which led to it forgotten. But apart from that, Liberality is hard to understand because, like its complement, Conservatism, it is not an abstract doctrine, and cannot be stated in a series of dogmas. If a man says he is a Mussulman, or a member of the Church of England, or a Communist, or a Roman Catholic, he professes certain definite doctrines and you know where to have him. But Liberality is not a doctrine; it is a spirit or attitude of mind, constantly changing in its outer manifestation according to the circumstances that it has to meet, but always essentially the same in itself, an effort to get rid of prejudice so as to see the truth, to get rid of selfish passions so as to do the right. It is not a popular attitude. The genuine Liberal wants to remedy injustice wherever he sees it, to correct the popular sentiments that are leading people astray. He befriends not the strong, but the weak, the suffering, those who cannot help themselves or him. He will help the voteless natives in Africa, the Jews in Germany and Poland, the racial minorities in Eastern Europe. He constantly runs the risk of being right but unpopular. A friend of mine heard an Albanian speak bitterly of a certain English Liberal. ''We thought he was a friend of Albania. When we were accused of murdering So-and-so he moved heaven and earth to get us tried and acquitted. But latterly, when we were accused of some murders in Epirus he turned against us.'' My friend pointed out that in the first case the accused were innocent, while in the second they were undoubtedly guilty, but the explanation only angered the Albanian. ''That is just like you English Liberals,'' he said. ''When we have a strong case you support us, and desert us when we are in real trouble!''

When a people's blood is up Liberality does not appeal to them. They call for something more instinctive, less rational. But further, apart from its lack of popular appeal, can the principle of Liberality in itself be defended. Does it allow for facts? Is it realistic? In answer to that doubt let us admit that in the management of any human society there is a mixture of right and of might, and that often it is practically necessary to acquiesce in injustice so as not to turn a burning house into a burning street. We cannot always go straight for righteousness as the crow flies. So much we may allow to Macchiavelli. But what we are asked for now is a concession quite different from that. Nietzsche tells us not that injustice or harshness is sometimes a regrettable necessity, but that "all high culture is based on cruelty," that "of all repulsive old women the quality of Humanity is the most repulsive, unless it be the other repulsive old woman, Truth."* Hitler describes humanitarianism as a "mixture of stupidity, cowardice, and superciliousness, which will melt away like snow in the March sunshine." He admits, however, that the pacifist-humane idea may be quite good when once the world has been thoroughly conquered by the Germans (*Mein Kampf*, p. 315). We can many of us remember Mussolini's glorifications of militarism, and the passionate eulogies of *brutalität*, especially towards pacifists and Jews, which distinguished the Nazi revolution.

These sentiments have little appeal in Great Britain. We neglect them as the ravings of neurotics, though we should remember that now, as once or twice before in history, neurotics on the throne may prove a very real danger. But a similar conclusion is sometimes urged on us by quite sane persons in France, America, and Britain on solemn grounds of evolutionist philosophy. "Evolution," argues the anti-Liberal mili-

* Quoted with approval by Maurras, *Action Française*, IV, p. 569.

tarist, "is simply the struggle for life. All life is a struggle. The weak fighters go to the wall, the strong fighters survive. Charity, generosity, chivalry, Liberality, are pretty ornaments on the surface of life, but when it comes to deadly realities nothing counts but fighting power."

Now in the vegetable world this is probably true. If two trees are competing for life in a piece of soil that is only enough for one the struggle is merciless and the best struggler wins. The mistake comes in transferring this analogy from the vegetable world, which has no brains and no social sympathies, to the animal world, which in its higher forms at any rate has both, and thence—Heaven help us!—even to human society. The doctrine goes dead against the views of the great evolutionists, such as Darwin and Herbert Spencer; it is explicitly refuted in Prince Kropotkin's remarkable book, *Mutual Help*. He makes it clear that even in the animal world the struggle for life is not a struggle of all against all, and the fittest to survive are by no means the most selfish and pugnacious. Long before you get as high as mankind the unit becomes a group, struggling partly indeed against other groups, but chiefly against difficulties of environment. Inside the group—and sometimes even between groups—there is need for the social qualities, for co-operation, for mutual help, for self-sacrifice. The *Illustrated London News* published some years ago a series of photographs showing the behaviour of various groups of gregarious animals faced with danger. It was practically always the same. The full-grown males in the front centre, facing the enemy, the younger males on the wings, the females behind in a ring and the young in the middle. And the enemy, one may remark, was never an animal of the same species; it was either man or some other of the predatory carnivores. By the time we come to man the group of course becomes larger and more complex. As civilization proceeds the element of fight diminishes, the element of mutual help increases. Present-day England probably spends a million pounds on social services for every few hundred it spends on the punishment of crime or rebellion; in the days of the Tudors the proportions were quite the reverse. Plato, after all, had the root of the matter; in every society, he says, there is an element of Force, βία, and an element of Persuasion, πειθώ; and the better the society, the more it depends on Persuasion and the less on Force.* That form of growth, and not a mere struggle for life, is the normal mode of human Evolution. No Government can remain a mere killing-machine.

"Ah, yes," our false evolutionist will object,

* *Laws*, p. 722.

"within the nation persuasion and mutual help may be the rule; between nations at any rate it is war, war ever increasing in effectiveness and ferocity." What is our answer? In the first place, this zoological analogy does not hold. A nation is not a natural unit like a herd of buffalo or a pack of wolves. It is largely an accidental unit. The Poles are a nation, but in the last war some Poles fought for Russia, some for Austria, and some for Germany. Was that a natural evolutionary process? And if, like Hegel, you take the state, not the nation, for your unit, how is it a natural evolutionary process that the Czechs as part of the Austrian Empire should be forced to fight for that empire until they got a chance of rebelling and fighting against it? In the second place, if we are to apply these zoological conceptions so crudely to human life, which group is the more natural and vital, the nation or the class? If in obedience to the natural struggle for life we are to encourage national wars surely we must encourage class wars as well. And between the two, even the most perverse evolutionist will admit, evolution will not evolve very far; there will not be much life left to struggle for.

It is clear, I think, that with the advance of civilization the element of mutual help within the group increases, and also that the social and moral feelings generated within the group extend their boundaries farther and farther. This is obviously, in both respects, a Liberalizing movement, and, no less obviously, a movement which all reasonable men accept as an advance in civilization. A society in which people carry on their family disputes by murdering one another or one another's relations is less advanced than one in which they accept a judge's decision. A country in which every clan is in a state of more or less permanent war against the next clan is less advanced than one which accepts, as a whole, the same law and social obligations. The only limits that I can admit to this process of pacification are the limits of practical possibility. Here, again, I frankly accept an ideal now terribly out of fashion, which was first proclaimed by my old Greek philosophers, inventors of the phrase κόσμου πολίτης, citizen of the world or ''cosmopolitan.'' They held that human society, rightly conceived, was not a chaos of warring interests, but a Cosmos, an ordered whole, in which every individual had his due share both of privilege and of service. The whole inhabited world was by rights one great City, not a discordant jumble of Greek and barbarian, or slave and free; not, as we might now say, a mere battleground of Fascist and Communist, or a mere mob of white, yellow, and black; one Great City of which all men are free citizens. And, lest that conception should seem, with all its idealism, to err on the material side, they added, using their own polytheistic language, "one great City of Men and Gods." Do not be repelled by the words; look to the meaning behind the words. Men, as they are, are miserably faulty beings. To make a true Cosmos, a true moral and spiritual order, there must be something higher in the world than men as we now know them; there must be those ideals and inspirations, that "something not ourselves making for righteousness," for which the ancients used their inadequate word θέοι, or "Gods."

People are fond of explaining that the League of Nations is only a League of *Nations*; it accepts the sovereign nation as a unit and a permanent necessity; it is not a superstate; not a federation; much less is it cosmopolitan. They tire me with these explanations. I agree, of course, that as things are the League has to be a League of Nations. In all its strictly political work it has to accept nations as they are, represented by their respective Governments, and to be very careful of offending their separate national ambitions and foolish vanities. This limitation gives a constant encouragement to old diplomats who do not like the League idea, to write to *The Times* and explain that any attempt at organizing justice between sovereign states is dangerous and impossible. But it is worth remembering that the League spends considerably more of its time on work that is non-political and therefore comparatively free from the moths and locusts of nationalism. The work of the Health Section, the Opium Section, the various humanitarian activities and most of the work on finance or communications and transit, is not only more successful than the political work but is conceived on a higher plane. The same is true of almost all the activities of the Organiza-tion of Intellectual Co-operation, in which I have worked for nearly twenty years. When we touch education or politics of course nationalism may block the path; but in the purely scientific work, in the co-operation between museums, universi-ties, archaeological institutes, and the like, the legal work affecting the rights of authors and artists, or the unemployment of intellectual workers; the better use of cinema and radio; even in the free discussions of the Committee of Arts and Letters, there is a genuine spirit of world co-operation. The United States and other non-members of the League play their part; Chinese and Japanese, Italian and French dele-gates debate together in a friendly spirit and our ship seldom strikes the reef of ''sovereignty.''

These disinterested activities of the League are not politics, and consequently are not much men-tioned in newspapers or attended to by Governments. But life implies growth, and if the League has life in it, as I believe it has, I see it developing in a measurable future towards that Federation of Europe which was advocated by Briand and Stresemann, and in a further and dimmer future, which may yet serve us as a guiding star, towards the One Great City of Men and Gods. That is the goal of civilization, the goal of Liberality.

I must apologize for that excursion into speculative philosophy. My Scottish blood at times runs away with me. Let us turn back, not to immediate practical politics, but to the principles of politics, and try to understand Liberality by contrast with Conservatism. In the first place, the two are not contrary principles; they are complementary. Neither is complete without the other. Neither is absolute or fanatical. Conservatism is an immensely important principle. It is based upon the truth that mankind in the civilized nations has by centuries of trial and error, experiment and struggle, built up a social order which is extremely precious and whose destruction would mean the loss of all that has been painfully won by the great reforms of the past. The object of Conservatism is to save the social order. The object of Liberality is to bring that order a little nearer to what the reformers aimed at and to what the judgment of a free man—free from selfishness, free from passion, free from prejudice—would require, and by that very change to save it the more effectively. The Conservative sees the importance of maintaining the strength and authority of his country, with its existing religion, social structure, and organs of government. He stresses the point that a faulty system which people like and understand often works better than a superior one which they do not want. The Liberal does not disagree, but feels more strongly that, if he wants to find what is really true and do what is really just he must be on his guard against the delusive powers of custom, prejudice, inertia, and the unconscious sleepless all-embracing egoism of his class and his nation. In one's judgment of any controversy the interests of one's own class, one's own nation, are always likely to carry too much weight. Even if there are no gross falsehoods uttered, the fact that one side of the controversy is always stated in full and listened to with sympathy, while the other is not heard, or not heard with patience, produces an enormous effect of unfairness.

The more I study the violent factions of Europe to-day, or even the party spirit of the average newspaper, the more I am convinced that there is no real substitute for truth, no substitute for justice. Sham substitutes are always offering themselves, which seem and are at the moment easier, simpler, more attractive, more deliciously intoxicating. Except when they themselves are wronged or slandered the mass of men as a rule care but coldly about strict truth or impartial justice. They prefer the myth that flatters them, the injustice that gives them an advantage over their rivals. It is commonly said that wars of religion have now ceased. Yet our wars are fought just as fanatically—and perhaps with as little sincerity—for rival mythologies. I doubt if it is really a genuine speculative belief in the theories of Fascism or Communism, Socialism or Capitalism, that produces these present torrents of hate and fear. You hate your enemy not because he differs from you about political theory: you hate him because you are afraid of him. You kill him because, if he can, he will kill you. The dogma or myth which you profess is, for the most part, an excuse to show how right you are and how wicked the enemy. "Our own people must be in the right:" the good citizen's beliefs must be adjusted to that main irresistible demand. History and reason must give way. This is the doctrine explicitly preached by Nietzsche and his followers, by the Governments in Germany and Italy, by the Nationalist Opposition in France: a deplorable human weakness exalted into a creed and an ideal.

In Nazi Germany it is necessary to believe that in 1914 an innocent German Government was treacherously attacked by envious enemies, that she won the war against immense odds, but in some mysterious way she was betrayed at the last moment by President Wilson, by the pacifists, by the civilians, by Jews, capitalists, and communists, and of course by the lying Allies. If that were not true Germany would be open to criticism; and Germany, the true German Germany, is above criticism. Nay more: Germany must have revenge for her wrongs; wrongs so colossal cannot be left unpunished. Therefore the guilty persons must be people in Germany's power. The English, the French, the Americans for the time being are out of reach; but the Jews are in reach and helpless. On them the nation's subterranean desires can be satisfied.

The Italian myth is in essentials similar. Why did Italy do so badly in the war? Why, after the victory, was Italy left impoverished and depressed, and even cheated out of some parts of the large accessions of foreign territory for which she had so pertinaciously bargained? *Ex hypothesi* it must not be Italy's fault; therefore it was because a corrupt and decadent world, dominated by unprincipled capitalists leagued with socialist revolutionaries—always the same curious combination!—had somehow poisoned the mind of Italy's leaders and reduced her social system to a weak legalism and parliamentarism; until at last a man arose, a man who was not afraid to shatter all rules and laws and paper treaties and the other devices of contemptible politicians and make Italy again a proud conquering nation. By his strong right arm he will re-create the old Roman temper and rebuild the old Roman Empire, and subject the decadent democracies to the new Augustus. The myth fills in the necessary details about British decadence, deceit, and barbarity, about French disorder and discontent, and the desire of all the Latin nations to take shelter under the wing of their strong Roman mother. It gives what is wanted; it satisfies the nation's desire, and if facts contradict it they can be suppressed.

So far as I have had conversations with Japanese nationalists they have a mythology of their own not very dissimilar. At present almost every civilized person outside Japan and the two nations that are by order pro-Japanese sees that the Japanese military party is committing a monstrous and inhuman aggression against China, in complete disregard of treaty obligations and common humanity. Practically everyone in Japan insists on believing that his country is fighting a heroic battle, after great provocation, for establishing peace in the East, punishing the deceitfulness of the Chinese, and checking the inroads of Communism. A myth has to be accepted or invented which will enable them to hold this belief: and this is duly done.

The Russian myth seems to be based on the resolute wish to believe that everything in the way of social reform was the invention of the Bolshevik revolution. A friend of mine who was being shown over a model school in Russia began to explain something about the system of national education in England. The courteous guide listened for a minute, but his patience then broke down. He could not listen to plain and obvious lies. Everyone knew that the working classes in England had no schools and were not allowed to read or write.* How far this myth is further diversified or fantasticated by stories of ubiquitous Fascist or Trotskyist plots is a question beyond my estimation.

Such myths of self-flattery or wish-appeasement are nothing new. Every nation is subject to them. Every nation starts with the assumption that it is God's own people, and is apt to add that it differs from all others by its superior honesty. But the ordinary democratic nation cannot produce anything like such large and well

* Compare a Russian account of English Education quoted below, p. 70.

ramified specimens as the totalitarian states with their rigid censorship and governmental myth-factories. In every country, hitherto, when these naïve delusions come into public notice, thoughtful men have always laughed at them or protested against them. What is new in the present totalitarian states is that for the first time the principle has been officially proclaimed that such delusions are the right things to uphold and to inculcate upon the young. The Germans, as usual, are most explicit and elaborate in this matter. They preach as philosophic theory what their Italian colleagues proclaim in threats and outbursts of passion. The Minister of Education himself at the great Heidelberg conference announced Nazi emancipation from ''the false idea of objectivity,'' and obedient to him the Professor of Philosophy at Heidelberg declared: ''We do not know of or recognize truth for truth's sake or science for science' sake.'' ''We will never approach history impartially,'' writes *Die Deutsche Schule*, ''but as Germans.'' History is not to be true history but German history; even physics, we hear from one of the greatest of Nazi scientists, Professor Stark, must henceforth be ''German physics,'' since pure physics have a taint of Einstein and Judaism about them. Together with the rejection of truth goes a rejection of justice. The reverence for moral right is a thing that "belongs to bygone times";* German youth should not bother about whether he is acting nobly or basely: the thing that matters is that he acts; in Dr. Goebbels' authoritative words, "What matters is not who is right but who wins." Especially between nations is any moral law out of place. "It smacks," as a leading Nazi once told me, "of Marxist ideology." The only good peace, writes Herr Hitler, is a "peace established by the victorious sword of a master nation" (*Mein Kampf*, p. 438). "No power on earth," says Mussolini, "shall stand between the Italian people and its will." Such a position is only reached, as the same authority has justly observed, by "trampling in the dust the rotting corpse of Liberalism." What part in such a world can those of us play for whom Liberality is not a rotting corpse but a living spirit? That is the problem to be treated in my next address.

* A publication of the *Deutscher Philologenband*, quoted by Ernst Wichert at the University of Munich, April 16, 1935.

*Liberality and
Civilization*

II

II

I wish in this second lecture to consider the problem of keeping alive liberal thought and feeling in a world which seems to have turned anti-liberal. Civilized thinking means liberal thinking. Liberality is the inner content of civilization. And as war, if it should come, is likely by its material destructiveness to wreck the material civilization of Europe from without, so the fear of war and memories of war by making liberality impossible are poisoning that civilization from within.

In speaking of war or the struggle to the death between man and man, one is confronted with the fact that, in itself, it may be either the vilest or the noblest of human activities. The man who faces death, fighting for a just cause and for those whom he loves is doing a noble act; ''greater love hath no man than this.'' The men who, for the sake of greed or ambition let loose their engines of destruction upon weaker victims, and then boast of the misery they have caused, have sunk to the lowest abysses of human crime. The main moral issue is clear enough, and has been clear for some thousands of years.* True, no class of men have enjoyed such adulation and glory as the great conquerors, quite irrespective of the rightness or wrongness of the cause for which they fought; Alexander, Julius Caesar, Frederick II, Napoleon, and all the rest of them. Yet against the glory there has always been heard a protest, the cry of suffering mankind against War as the great evil, clear enough in Erasmus, in William Penn, in Kant and others, but never, I think, more deep and heart-rending than over two thousand years ago in certain passages of Homer and Aeschylus, and above all in the *Trojan Women* of Euripides. Like Slavery and certain other scourges of mankind, the evil has long been recognized and divers remedies speculatively suggested, but none have been widely accepted as feasible until our own day. The reason for this is twofold.

In the first place, although an obvious evil, War was never an all-embracing and intolerable

* In the oldest of all Greek tragedies we find laid down, not as an original idea but as part of the traditional moral code, a plea for international arbitration: first a prayer for the citizens among whom there "reigns with Brotherhood foreseeing Thought": then, more remarkable, and equally clear:

"To strangers and strange lands let them afford,
    Without long strife, Law and the healing Word,
    And Justice grant ere any draw the sword."
                    (Aeschylus, *Suppliant Women*, 700 ff.)

evil, absolutely incompatible with the continuance of civilization, until the present century. It is surprising to the present generation of Europeans, when reading about famous wars in the past or remote and ill-equipped wars in the present, to learn how limited they were in the numbers engaged, in geographical extent, and in what one may call penetration below the surface. The armies destroyed everything in their path, but the path was narrow, and towns a little way out of the path were hardly affected. During the Chinese civil war the Holt company, so one of the partners told me, imported several million eggs from the centre of hostilities, and few or none were broken. We can scarcely believe, at first, that Miss Austen was writing her placid novels all through the heat of the Napoleonic Wars; or that English cloth merchants were regularly and admittedly providing the uniforms for the French armies. We rub our eyes to read in a letter of Gibbon's that this time he really thinks he will travel to England from Geneva via Ostend instead of going through France as usual, since "the long war has rendered even that polite people somewhat peevish." It is only of late that the power of Governments has so increased as to enable them to lay hands on the bodies of the whole nation as *matière conscriptable* and the wealth of the whole nation as a war fund. Add to these considerations the immense increase in destructive power put at the State's disposal by modern engineering and chemistry, and one sees that the word "war" now denotes an extremely different thing from the wars of past centuries.

Thus the first reason for this great effort made now, as it was never made before, to exterminate war from the civilized world, is that modern civilization has vastly increased the extent of the evil. The second reason is that modern civilization has also made practicable a degree of concerted action for the promotion of peace which was never possible before. I need hardly dwell on this point. It is not merely that the increased powers of communication and the ever-growing social and economic nexus makes possible and almost inevitable an organized world-wide effort towards establishing a unity of civilization and thus indirectly making war unprofitable and even ridiculous: I think we must also recognize the influence of the moral advances made by civilized man in the nineteenth century, the awakening of his social conscience and the ever-widening range of his imaginative sympathy, as shown by the great humanitarian efforts to relieve suffering, and the uncomprehending horror with which most of us—even after our recent experiences— hear about the deliberate cruelties of the law in previous times or see in museums the old instruments of torture.

No doubt this increased moral sensitiveness may be largely due to mere material conditions: the decrease of crime to greater publicity and better lighting of the streets; the horror of inflicting or contemplating pain to the invention of anaesthetics. But it would, I think, be mere blindness not to recognize the existence of it, and in particular of a sincere and passionate revolt of the human conscience against what is felt as the wickedness involved in war. This moral sensitiveness may be passing away under the deadening influence of the atrocities to which we are now inured. But in England it is still immensely strong, and I notice that even in the militarist totalitarian States a continuous governmental propaganda is found necessary in order to break it down.

Let us first remind ourselves what form any effort after peace was bound to take. The fugitives from anarchy in ancient times, we remember, found a way to live by building a *Polis*, a City Wall, within which they were safe and, being safe, however different their histories and origins, they could all form a Society. Outside the wall were wild beasts and enemies; inside the wall was the rule of law and the cementing influence of friendship and common interests. Is there any way by which the fugitives from our modern anarchy, the anarchy of a world-civilization governed by sixty-odd independent self-determining governments, could build their *Polis* and form themselves into a unity? Clearly no single state is at present strong enough to impose unity on a subject world. The old Roman solution is out of the question. Can there be a voluntary federation of all civilized, or even of all European States, each one abandoning its independent sovereignty and putting full faith in the federal authority? Out of the question too; at any rate for the present. States are losing their sovereignties bit by bit—Heaven be praised!—and, as long as they do not notice it, all goes well. Every new treaty or "commitment" nibbles away some fragment of the cherished right of every State to do as it likes, irrespective of the rights or welfare of other States; and such treaties are now made, literally, by the hundred where fifty years ago they could be counted in dozens. But as things stand, it is clear enough that no State will permit its own policy to be settled by a foreign majority on an international council. It may allow itself to be persuaded; it will not allow itself to be dictated to. These limitations practically decide the form which must be taken by any international effort to prevent a recurrence of war. I have seen a very large number of

schemes for the Enforcing of Peace, the Out-
lawry of War, and the like, both before the
Covenant was made and after; I have studied
many proposals for the amendment of the
Covenant itself. But it is curious how, when one
considers both what is desired and what is practicable, the result of the various schemes is almost
always the same. It is not practicable to get
nations to abandon their independence; hence
world federations and the like are ruled out. Yet,
since the thing that is desired is security, no
arrangement which does not in some sense protect its members against war is worth wasting
time upon. The solution inevitably is a Society of
Nations, inside which the Members will observe
law, justice, and the ordinary habits of friendship
one with another, not merely renouncing War
themselves but accepting the principle that an
attack on any one member is an attack upon all.
If it is at all true, as we most of us believed at
the end of the World War and as President
Roosevelt declared on October 14, 1937, that
90 per cent of the peoples of the world want
peace and only some 10 per cent want to disturb
the peace, the solution laid down in Article XVI
of the Covenant would seem to be as absolutely
right in practice as it is in ethics. That principle
is what the President describes as ''quarantine.''
The nation, or Government, which is infected

with the poison of aggressive warmongering should be isolated from the uninfected world. Rather more clearly, if less picturesquely, the Covenant, which is based on co-operation between members of the League in all good and lawful purposes, lays down the rule of absolute non-co-operation in the crime of aggressive war. As soon as any Government is convicted of committing or preparing that international crime, the rest are to withdraw all their co-operation, in whatever manner and to whatever degree may be most wise and effectual; to exclude its goods from their ports; to sell it no arms, no oil, no metals, no materials of war. There has never yet been the slightest difficulty in determining the aggressor; and in a world of which 90 per cent or even 70 per cent really wished to put an end to war, not merely to escape war themselves while helping other nations to destroy each other, such refusal of co-operation would be absolutely effective. No doubt it demands a sacrifice from each nation; the economic sacrifice of losing trade, and the diplomatic sacrifice of preferring the friendship of a weak nation to that of a strong. It implies indeed a higher general standard of international liberality; and nothing irritates the average man more than a demand that he should be more liberal. Yet nations would surely be ready to make even that sacrifice if, in return, they could really be secured against the risk of war. They can be free from war if they like, and we know that to be so was the prayer of the whole world in 1918. The startling fact that confronts us is that, even after the horrors of the Great War, this world-wide longing for peace and good will among the warring and suffering tribes of men has not merely flagged in its intensity: it has been met by an assertion of the opposite principle, an absolute rejection of the moral law between nations, and an acceptance of the rule of pure force, more conscious, explicit, and all-embracing than ever before in human history.

If we ask how this anti-moral, anti-legal, anti-constitutional revolution arose, we must remember that the ordinary official world was, as a matter of fact, not ready for the League system. Old diplomats, skilled and experienced in the arts of mildly bullying the weak, cajoling the strong, and snatching national advantage out of other nations' troubles, seem scarcely able to believe that the Covenant was really meant to be acted upon. You can see it from their letters to *The Times*. More than that, we must remember that the worship of force is not only a tradition in the dreams of unregenerate man, but that in some societies, such as the ancient Spartans, the Japanese Samurai, and the ruling classes of

Prussia, it has always been a cherished article of faith. But its special virulence in the present post-war period came, I think, from the war itself and what seemed to people's war-heated imaginations a sudden discovery of the utter unrighteousness of the existing world order and the hypocrisy of what was accepted as law.

It began where there was the greatest excuse, in the Bolshevik revolution in Russia. I do not wish to embark on the merits and demerits of the Russian revolution. That is a highly controversial subject. Probably most people would agree that among all the violent revolutions of this century that in Russia had the most excuse, committed the worst excesses, and achieved the most remarkable results; but I want to dwell upon one point only. Most revolutions are based on some disillusionment, the rejection of some conventional imposture. Now in Russia this disillusionment, this rejection, was more complete than anywhere else in modern history. A people that had been superstitiously trustful and obedient under a very corrupt system, found themselves cynically betrayed by those whom they trusted, and dragged through morasses of wrong and suffering which surpass description. So when they rebelled they rebelled against the whole established social order. They rejected not merely the Czar, the Orthodox Church, and the landowners, but all religion, all conventions, all the current ideals of justice and humanity. In Lenin's famous phrase the question became simply "*Who Whom?*", that is, "Which shall destroy the other?"; and the instrument—borrowed in idea from Marat, who wanted as a foundation for his reforms the heads of thirty thousand aristocrats—was the appalling instrument of "mass terror." As things have turned out, the Russian Revolution has, in its foreign relations at least, proved far more easily compatible with the ordinary principles of civilization than was expected in its early years. The Union of Soviet Republics can now, it would seem, be reckoned as a force working on the side of peace. But historically the Bolshevik outbreak is a cardinal instance of that sudden rejection of the existing social order and all its values which makes revolutions. "All men are liars; all so-called justice is injustice. I and my comrades have been tortured beyond the limit; therefore we recognize no law and are out to destroy." Mr. Branting, the Swedish Prime Minister, once told me he had asked Lenin in 1915 or 1916 what ideas he had for reconstruction after he had destroyed the social order of Russia; Lenin said he must leave that to others. His work was to destroy.

The war worked differently in every country,

All had their grievances, all had what is more important, their temptations, their self-justifying myths. The Russians, maddened by the war itself, turned against their military caste. The Germans, maddened by their defeat after continual victories, blamed for it not their military caste, but all who, at home or abroad, had been that caste's enemies. Their real grievance was, and is, their defeat in the Great War: but their disillusion was completed by the lofty professions of the League of Nations compared with the real actions of its leading members. The Japanese, deeply hurt by the denial of their claim to race equality and elated by successful conquests, wanted more conquests. The Italians, somewhat humiliated by their war experiences, finding their appetite for territory stimulated rather than satisfied by their gains, and their emigration to America rudely curtailed, fell under the influence of an ambitious and masterful adventurer. But the result in all four countries has been curiously similar. Both the German and the Italian dictators have accepted Lenin's doctrine of "*Who Whom?*" Both reject the whole idea of justice or morality between nations, and the Japanese, though less articulate, have in act been equally thorough and deservedly earned their Nazi title of "honorary Aryans." "Either the world will be governed by the ideology of modern democracy," says Hitler in *Mein Kampf* . . . "or it will be ruled by the laws of force, when the people of brutal determination, not those that show self-restraint, will triumph" (p. 148). "The struggle between two worlds can permit no compromise," says Mussolini; "either we or they: either their ideas or ours." And the context shows that the conflict between the ideas is to be decided by the cutting of throats, not by argument. Civilized nations conduct their foreign policy by methods of co-operation, of friendly discussion; when necessary by compromise or arbitration. But Dr. Goebbels, who speaks with the highest authority, says: "The only instrument with which one can conduct foreign policy is alone and exclusively the sword."* And though the particular passages

* References in *We or They*, by H. F. Armstrong (Macmillan, 1937). I might add evidence of the new tone in education inculcated in the Nazi school books; a history freed from the "curse of objectivity" is to teach children "the exclusive recognition of the right of their own people" (A. Viernow, *Zur Theorie und Praxis des nationalsozialistischen Geschichtsunterrichts*) and "the Race question raised to a dominant place" (*Mein Kampf*, p. 471); arithmetic for children is to dwell largely on calculations about bombing planes; and even grammar distorted into abuse of pacifists and Jews (R. Alschner, *Sprachkundliche Kleinarbeit im neuen Geiste*). Russian teaching seems to be not nearly so anti-moral in theory, but to content itself with extreme anti-capitalist propaganda. See an article in *The Times* of November 13, 1937. The text book quoted explains that British

were expunged in 1933 after they had served their purpose, neither France nor other peace-loving countries can be expected to forget the well-known words in which the present Head of the German Reich, in a book which is all-but compulsory reading for all the nation, explains not merely the necessity for the "annihilation of France," but the necessity for regarding the destruction of France not as an end but as a beginning (*Mein Kampf*, pp. 766, 699, 757).

Now there is nothing absolutely new in these views. The Hitler movement is no doubt blatant and uneducated compared with the old German militarism of 1914. But, not to speak of Nietzsche and Treitschke, much the same sentiments can be found in the works of Count Reventlow, who was the oracle of pre-war Prussian militarism,

colonists, ten times as numerous as the inhabitants of the mother land, are "struggling for their independence"; conditions in mines, etc., are described as they were a hundred years ago, and Dickens' account of Dotheboys Hall used to show what schools are in capitalist countries. I do not know Russian textbooks, but I have read in a geography textbook of another country that only 5 per cent of the English can read or write, and that they largely feed upon raw beef, "which accounts for their brutality." I showed the book to a colleague of mine from the country in question, who burst out laughing and secured the withdrawal of the textbook from the schools. The state in question was not totalitarian.

and he was not writing under the infuriating influence of defeat. One must always allow for that. I often recall the French feelings of fury and despair after 1870, and tremble to think what the state of mind of our own people would be if, after some eight centuries of peace and confident security, we had been beaten in the Great War.

There is nothing very new, nothing unintelligible, but there is in the prevalence of these sentiments a terrible breaking loose of *la bête humaine*; a terrible failure of European Liberality and the hopes of the League of Nations.

War, as usual, has taught the world its two contradictory lessons. All wars teach them; but the World War of 1914 to 1918 being greater than any of its predecessors has spread its teaching more widely and enforced it more deeply. Part of the world learnt that war means common misery and mutual destruction. Nations can destroy one another if they will; they can save one another if they will. But no one nation can destroy the others and save itself. They learnt the lesson of peace. But another part learnt a simpler lesson: that *inter arma silent leges*. When once the guns begin to fire law and justice do not matter. Put against each other a man with good arguments and a man with a gun, and the gun wins every time. In all disputes violence, not reason or justice, is ultimately the trump card; and, that being so, why waste your breath on argument? Why not play your trump at once. A friend of Signor Mussolini told me with admiration how that great man, when still a private citizen, just after the war, put an end to an agricultural strike. He went with a little band of his Arditi to speak to a group of the strike leaders; the latter began to argue their case, Mussolini said, "Go and milk those cows"; they continued to argue, he made a sign and the Arditi cut the strikers' throats. He then proceeded to another group, using the same methods, and the cows were promptly milked. The strike was over.

Do not let us dwell on the physical horrors of war. They are dwelt upon quite enough already. And do not let us make the mistake of thinking that war, because it is illiberal and materially disastrous and productive of misery and crime, has not a moral side to it and does not offer a great field for virtue. To use violence against the right is wicked; but to stand up against violence for the sake of the right is noble. Let us not forget, either, that these totalitarian revolutionary movements, amid all their violence and stupidity, have in them a strong element of moral reform: a burning idealism, however misguided, a spirit of faith and hope, however hysterical; a habit of discipline and self-sacrifice which the ordinary traditional and constitutional democracies often greatly need and seldom seem able to practise. The tragedy of the situation is that this intensity of purpose is directed towards ends incompatible with human welfare. But let that be as it may. I wish for the moment to consider how war, whatever its other qualities, is essentially and necessarily illiberal and contrary to civilization.

I see two fundamental reasons. First, the liberal and civilized mind is essentially disinterested, the war-mind necessarily partisan. A liberal man, free from prejudice and passion, sees that the welfare of all human beings is good: it may be his first business to attend to the welfare and health of the people of Bristol, or Birmingham, or Glasgow, but he quite sees that the health of the people of Paris or Berlin is desirable. But war begins by regarding some mass of people as enemies, whose welfare is an evil, whose suffering, maiming, misery, and death are things to procure and rejoice over. The enemy may number hundreds of millions as in 1914 to 1918; he may be only a small tribe across the frontier. But the principle is the same. And it is a principle utterly contrary to liberality or civilization.

Secondly, war introduces into human action a motive of irresistible strength. If war comes you are fighting for your life; you are confronted by

the greatest evils possible; you are using the very
last ounce of your physical strength, the last
extreme effort of your ingenuity to achieve one
definite object, the defeat of the enemy; and no
minor considerations of ethics or humanity can
be allowed to blunt your action. These infinite
motives are always dangerous; even when it is
only a saint's entirely laudable desire to save his
own soul, or a Jesuit's partially laudable desire
at all costs to uphold his Church. But when the
infinite motive is of such very ambiguous moral
value as the desire to do the maximum of evil
to your enemy in order to save your own people,
the clash with the ethics of any free man becomes
violent.

The problem of living a Christian life in an un-
Christian world is one with which the Churches
have been familiar ever since they came into
being. There is a similar problem facing the
Liberal living in an illiberal world; and seldom
can it have been more acute than now. "War,"
as Thucydides says, "is a violent master and
teaches by compulsion." And the lessons are
taught not only by the actual war when it is
present, but by the preparations that come before
it and the memories that are left behind.

Let me take two examples of the utter and
fundamental discord between the lessons of war
and the thoughts of any free man. During the

Great War the Germans tried to starve us and we more successfully tried to starve the Germans. That was ordinary enough. It was part of the normal methods of war. Then came an extension of it. Poland, most unhappy of European nations, was swept by alternate armies, conquered by the Germans, devastated and laid bare. The Poles were our allies. Our newspapers had accounts of the appalling distress in Poland—the roads strewn with skeletons, the almost complete blotting out of children under seven, and the like. The Americans proposed to send food for the relief of the Poles. But we made objection. We did not allow food to go into Poland, to save our own allies, who were starving. Why? Because the Germans were still taking from the miserable country all the food they could wring out of it, and if the Americans brought in more food, undoubtedly the enemy would take more. There was no choice. The "violent master" applied his compulsion. The Admiralty had to prohibit the entry of the food ships. But the man who had to sign that order may well have wished he had died before the need came to him.

That lesson belongs to the moral distortions produced by war itself. But the fear or the purpose of war, the mere presence of what is called a war mentality, is equally the direct and deadly enemy of all that a free man believes and lives for.

Let me take the case of a very noble nation now poisoned by the war-spirit, Japan.

"In order to conquer the world," said the famous Tanaka memorandum presented to the Emperor in 1927, "we must first conquer China." A vast undertaking, considering the size of China, but at one time made possible by its civil wars, its brigandage, its lack of unity, and the helplessness of its Governments against flood, famine, and pestilence. But meantime a change has set in. China is becoming united. North and South are beginning for the first time to feel the same patriotism and even to speak the same dialect. More dangerous still, China is in the early stages of a great renaissance. The Nanking Government has been vigorously putting down the opium traffic; it is conducting with the help of the League of Nations a great and successful work of education in agriculture, engineering, and above all in public health. It is building roads, embankments, and railways. It has established several universities. There is a new enthusiasm in the air. China will perhaps, under an effective and enlightened government, become a great united country, peaceful and prosperous, and conscious of its high traditions. "That will never do," says the war-mind of Japan. "We must prevent the recovery of the Chinese. Let us wreck their finances by a vast campaign of smuggling protected by our ships of war. Better still, let us start in China, through our own factories and shops, under protection of our armies, a vast trade in opium. That will not only provide a revenue for our armies of occupation, it will ruin the health, morale, and self-respect of the Chinese and make them an easier prey. Better still, let us import heroin, which is more destructive than opium and will weaken them more." (Those who have read Russell Pasha's report on this subject will not easily forget its horrors.) "Then at a suitable time we can pick a quarrel, destroy the universities, agricultural institutes, and medical schools, exterminate the leaders of the renaissance, and whether we annex great provinces or not, we shall at least have crippled our enemy, destroyed his hopes, and saved our beloved Japan!" Accepting the assumptions of the war-mind, the argument seems to me logical. It is difficult, here as always, to disentangle the desire for aggression from the fear of being attacked. They are always mixed or fused in the militarist mind. But my point is that as soon as you accept the assumptions of that mind you must oppose almost everything that a free-minded man calls good. You may be a hero; but you are likely to be a devil. I have chosen extreme instances. In slighter and less devilish forms this pervertive influence is at work everywhere.

It is the same in all branches of social life. Wider freedom of trade and intercourse is seen to be in the interest of the world not only by every Liberal but by every competent economist. Every economic conference, from the World Conference of 1927 onwards, calls for a lowering of trade barriers and more liberal treatment of refugees and immigrants. But the countries under the influence of the war-mind do not care about world prosperity, do not care much even about their own people's prosperity; they want to be sure that in case of war they shall not be dependent in any way on their neighbours. To the war-mind neighbours are all potential enemies. So they plunge into the labyrinths of autarky, or still worse, into the prison of totalitarianism.

The essential criticism to pass on these "dictatorships" is contained in that word itself. A dictator was an ancient Roman commander-in-chief, created for the immediate needs of war and compelled to lay down his office as soon as the war was over. A totalitarian State is a permanent dictatorship, a State in which the war neurosis is permanently established. In war time there has to be a censorship on news from the front, otherwise the enemy might learn things that we wish to conceal. In war time there has even to be a censorship on the expression of thought: thoughts are violent at such a time, and their free expression might cause mutinies or discouragement. But under a totalitarian government all news is war news, all knowledge and speculation is seen chiefly in its bearing on war, and all thoughts are apt to be violent thoughts. Such a government is afraid of all thought, of all knowledge, of all that distracts the mind from the main preoccupation—War. The whole range of knowledge must be censored, garbled, and suppressed.*

Again, every free man assumes, as a matter of course, that research should be free; if not free to discover truth it is meaningless. Every free man feels an imperative need, from time to time, to reflect on his own actions: to try to make sure that what he does is right and not wrong, that what he believes is true and not a delusion. But to the war-minded government free research seems dangerous, and moral sensitiveness absolutely intolerable. Who knows what the human intellect may discover? Who knows what the human conscience may say? When so much has to be concealed, it is safer to have a people with no conscience, no religion, and no intellect. It

* See for example in the *Kriegswirtschaftliche Jahresberichte*, 1936, 1937, articles by Professor Forsthoff, ''Kriegswirtschaft und Sozialverfassung,'' and by the editor, Dr. K. Hesse, on ''Die menschliche Arbeitskraft in der Kriegswirtschaft.''

is probably this permanent all-embracing denial of freedom, more than the accompanying acts of physical brutality, which constitutes the deepest and most enduring wrong inflicted by these dictatorships on the human spirit.

Let me take a few instances of the same clash of principles from the experience of my own League of Nations committee, the Committee of Intellectual Co-operation, some trifling, some serious. One of the earliest projects that our scientific experts discussed was a chart of the air, at different altitudes, indicating the prevalent air currents, as a chart of the ocean shows the ocean currents. An obviously useful scheme for civil aviation. It was promptly vetoed by certain Governments on military grounds. Better the air over their own country should be as unknown as possible! Who can blame them?

A convention has been drawn up by our committee concerning the use of one of the great new methods of diffusing knowledge, the radio. It is a modest effort, but binds the signatories to use this powerful instrument in the service of peace and good will between nations, to give objective news and avoid broadcasts calculated to cause offence or breed discord. It has been generally accepted and signed by many Governments. And all the time the official Italian station at Bari has been sending out in Arabic broadcast messages to the Moslem nations, preaching the downfall of the British Empire, encouraging discontent, and expounding the theme that when Islam wants a champion against British tyranny Mussolini with his famous Islamic sword—made in Italy—is ready and waiting.* Quite a useful measure for weakening the British Empire before the struggle begins. Much the same criticism can be passed on the German wireless broadcasts to South America. After all, an optimist may say, "These mendacious broadcasts in the end defeat themselves. The truth is bound to filter in from other nations." But no: for the purposes of future war it is not only desirable that the false propaganda should be issued; the true news is also carefully shut out. It would seem impossible

* "The Italian Broadcasting Company is to increase from December 1st the number of talks transmitted in foreign languages. Talks in Arabic, which hitherto have been transmitted once or twice weekly, are now to become a daily feature of the programme of two stations, 2RO (short wave) and Bari (medium wave), while a broadcast in Hindustani will be transmitted every Saturday by the former. News is to be transmitted in Chinese, Japanese, Serbian, Greek, Portuguese (for Latin America), Turkish, Rumanian, and Albanian, as well as in the chief European languages" (*The Times* Correspondent in Rome, November 21, 1937). "The Nazi Government's arrangements for fomenting disaffection in various parts of the British Empire are even more complete and *wissenschaftlich*" (*Manchester Guardian*, January 15, 1938).

to do this, but it can be done. I know a lady who was in Russia during the revolution and for five years after: during the whole of those five years she and all her acquaintances were under the impression that Germany had won the war. One could cite many examples to show that the German and Italian Governments are not less efficient than the Russian either in censorship or invention.

Take, again, another activity of Intellectual Co-operation which no German is allowed to attend and Italians look at askance, the International Studies Conference. It is a Conference of experts in international problems, drawn from our own Royal Institute of International Affairs and its "opposite numbers" in twenty-eight different countries. They choose a subject, divide it up among their various members, study it intensively for two years, exchange their papers, and then meet to discuss and publish their results. Two years ago the subject was "Collective Security," this year it was "Peaceful Change"; two years hence it will be "Economic Policies in Relation to World Peace." These are all ques- tions of vital importance: they must sooner or later be settled under pain of disaster. Yet they are not ripe for settlement by Governments, and in some ways are too delicate or too much charged with emotion for official international discussion. The International Studies Conference forms the ideal instrument for their preliminary study. Its international character is essential. No purely national body can escape onesidedness, or at least the suspicion of onesidedness. The two years' study by experts works wonders. Many national prejudices and violent emotions are removed as soon as the disputants have before them the actual facts, well ascertained and not open to contradiction.

Take, again, our Advisory Committee on League of Nations Teaching, or, as it is now called, "On the Teaching of the Facts and Principles of International Co-operation." This Committee has had a fine though chequered career. In the year 1924, on the initiative of the British Government, the Assembly of the League of Nations passed unanimously a resolution emphasizing "*the fundamental importance of familiarizing young people throughout the world with the principles and work of the League of Nations, and of training the younger generation to regard international co-operation as the normal method of conducting world affairs.*" A committee was set up with the purpose of carrying out this work: every year at the Assembly there were interested debates and unanimous votes for the furtherance of education on these lines. I remember vividly conversations I had with the Education Ministers of Central

American and Balkan countries, and the enthusiasm with which this scheme was greeted by the teachers of one country after another. The British teachers carried it out with great efficiency. The National Association of French Elementary Teachers passed resolutions recognizing "their duty as educators to make every effort to lead the younger generation to the knowledge and understanding of other peoples in order thus to contribute to the organization of peace." The teachers "undertook to abstain in their teaching from any word that may be injurious to international understanding," and to eschew all schoolbooks which tended in a contrary direction. Meantime in Germany itself, even in the first bitterness of a lost war, the authors of the Weimar Constitution had risen to a conception no less noble in spirit: "In every school the educational aim must be moral training, public spirit, personal and vocational fitness, and above all the cultivation of the German national character and the spirit of international reconciliation." In Prussia under the guidance of the Socialist Minister, Dr. Becker, the work was especially good. The breath of this liberal spirit, it seemed, had gone out over the whole world. When the C.I.C. made an inquiry into the movement, so marked in France, England, and America, for the re-writing of history textbooks in a more objective and less nationalist tone, we were astonished at the volume of answers that came rolling in from almost every country in the world.* The whole of mankind seemed to be shaken from its dogmatic slumber.

And then came the Hitler revolution. The Weimar Constitution was thrown on the scrap-heap, and with it, not only in Germany but in many countries, the whole educational effort of the League. I need not repeat the quotations, few out of many, that I made in the first of these addresses, from German and Italian authorities. There is a certain country, not long emancipated from Turkish rule, where in 1924, so the Minister of Education told me, the Government being too poor to build the schools that were clamoured for, the peasants themselves in two thousand villages had in their spare hours cut down trees in the national forests and built schools in which this new education from the West might be brought to them. A few years ago I asked a professor from that country what sort of international training his students received, and he answered simply, "My students are trained to be mad dogs."

It is rare, of course, to find in this "mad-dog" teaching much actual glorification of war; it

* The chief exceptions were perhaps Italy and Russia in Europe, and China and Japan (who were practically at war) in the Far East.

breaks out occasionally, as when German youths are told to devote themselves to ''St. Michael, the Angel of Destruction''—a title which would have surprised the saint—or when little Italian boys are taught to revel in the niceties—if I may so misapply the word—of bayonet drill. That is not the customary way in which the evil spirit works on a people; what he does is to flatter and stimulate their national egotism, their pride, their claims and ambitions, till at last they feel a sense of intolerable wrong that a race so obviously chosen by God to dominate the earth should be baulked of its legitimate desires. I doubt if there was ever a war-monger in modern times, from Frederick to William II, who did not explain that he desired nothing but peace—provided, of course, that his just demands were granted.

Finally, there is one great repentance incumbent on an illiberal world, not directly due to war or the fear of war, though stimulated into action by that experience. In looking through the blood-stained history of modern civilization one can find no darker crime than the treatment of what are commonly called the ''lower'' races by the ''higher,'' or, more accurately speaking, of the races without the resources of modern civilization by those who possess them. The slave trade, the extermination, complete or partial, of the Incas, the North American Indians, the native Australians; the horrors of the Congo and the Putumayo, are all matters of notoriety. They all begin, as the Greeks would say, with *Hubris,* a sense of overweening arrogance on the part of the stronger, and a contempt for people whom they do not trouble to understand. To take one instance out of many: the native Australians are still in the Stone Age, pre-agricultural, pre-pastoral; they are sometimes termed the lowest types of humanity. But I well remember my father long ago maintaining that for honesty and truthfulness he would sooner trust a native than a white man, and that in all the matters in which they had experience, such as wood-craft, tracking, knowledge of plants, birds, and beasts, their intelligence was at least equal to ours. They have since shown that it is much the same in such subjects as languages and mathematics. Yet I can remember when these people were with impunity shot at sight or exterminated like vermin by the scattering of poisoned meat and poisoned flour. That was long ago. The repentance has begun. Under the Australian and Papuan Governments at any rate magnificent amends are being made. But it remains generally true that wherever white man, uncontrolled by a disinterested public opinion, has dealings with a race which his own arms and wealth have put utterly at his mercy, the old abuses spring up again, and whole masses of human beings, poverty-stricken, starving, and helpless, linger on in what the League Commission terms "conditions akin to slavery." The rebellion of the world's conscience against these conditions was expressed by General Smuts in Article XXII of the Covenant and the institution of the Mandates Commission. The voice of Liberality was at last heard, proclaiming that no man, and certainly no race, is good enough to be absolute master of another; and that if these weaker races are to be our concern at all they must be so, not as mere "living tools" or sources of profit but as "a sacred trust of civilization."

Here, again, we meet the liberal gospel of the war-schooled world, and here, again, its utter denial and the proclamation of the opposite doctrine. Japan freely ignores her mandate; the German Press, with utter contempt, when demanding the return of the colonies, repudiates any proposal of a mandate; one of the latest Nazi books, starting from the accepted hocus-pocus about the pure-blooded Nordic man, deduces therefrom the necessity of the institution of slavery. Meantime Mr. Pirow in South Africa is welcoming the idea of German co-operation and advocating in sinister terms the establishment of "a uniform system of dealing with the natives"—

a system which would, I fear, be very different from that approved in this country.

There is the liberal reform and there is its denial. Apart from moral considerations can civilization continue if it is denied? The people who once had no weapons and were utterly at our mercy are now acquiring them. The Japanese, once helpless against us, are now armed only too well; the Chinese are being forced to arm; the Afghans have their fleet of aeroplanes. The Australians, of course, can be starved out without difficulty, but the Africans are being trained by French and Italian masters in the elements of military tactics and the use of the rifle, and by a thousand causes, personal and impersonal, in a dread and hatred of the white man. If we wish peace and civilization to continue there is no alternative to justice, there is no alternative to Liberality.

The modern world is dominated by fear—fear created by the Great War and perpetuated by its consequences and memories. The fear is justified —that is the terrible thing—yet it must be conquered, for, as it spreads, fear becomes the root of so many evils. For us who believe in Liberality as a living spirit the task that lies ahead, however difficult, is one about which we must try to think clearly. Some ways that seem to entice us are clearly wrong. We must not become the pupils of the militarists, and through our indignation against militarism, acquire the war-mind ourselves. We must not become their victims by submitting to their will, acquiescing in their outrages, and trying to coax them into the League of Nations by abandoning all that the League of Nations means. We must not become—and that is the greatest danger—a mixture of pupil and victim; harshly militarist about our own immediate interests or rights and indifferent or submissive about those of the rest of the world. Neither can we fly for refuge to pure pacifism. If we believe that sacrifice is good let us at least sacrifice ourselves, not our neighbours. To undertake solemnly, and with an air of religious duty, never to defend your brother against wrong if the wrongdoer uses armed force, seems to me to be a denial not only of liberality but of civilization itself. No. The only safe road is a straight road. On a straight road no one ever lost his way. The nations that for the sake of peace are ready to live according to law and accord justice to others are a vast majority. They have vast economic and military strength. Their united will would be, I think, irresistible, so long as it operates along peaceful channels for liberal and lawful ends. But they are not united. They have not earned one another's trust. Few Governments of the present day are genuinely liberal in spirit; their peoples, I believe, are ready to follow a nobler lead but are not receiving it.

Refugees amid this new return of ancient savagery, we nations that believe in civilization must build our city wall, we must form that *Polis* which men build in order to live, and keep rebuilding and re-forming in order to live well. We must make that city safe from dangers without. The way is shown by the Covenant of the League, reinforced during these last months by the President of the United States and the Secretaries of State of both the great American parties. Nations can only live by co-operation; without co-operation their roots are cut from under them. If the great majority of the nations want peace, let them co-operate with one another in the things of peace; let them refuse absolutely to co-operate with the makers of war, and war presently will be impossible. Let us make the world-city safe from danger without, and bit by bit we can free it from grave injustice within. Meantime it is worth remembering that the injustices that make men mad are often trifling things, daily irritations, slights to their pride, denials of their hopes, all of which can be relieved without any menace to the foundations of society by the spirit of liberality and brotherhood, and by what John Bright called "Justice the miracle-worker."

All this can be done provided the world has security; provided it can get free from the war-mind; provided the 90 per cent who desire peace and are ready for justice can make their will prevail. But can they? Let us look not at one particular country, but on our modern civilization as a whole. That great civilization, perhaps the greatest there has ever been, unparalleled in material resources, professing for the most part Christian principles, is still staggering under the blow of 1914 to 1918 and threatened with more deadly blows still. It can save itself. It knows the right way and has bound itself by treaties to follow it. But has it the will-power, the conscience, the vitality? Is it a living tree capable of putting forth new branches and strong ones after its great wound, or is it for the most part dead wood that, once broken, stays broken permanently?

The Governments of certain great nations have chosen a path which, to the eyes of most of us here, seems the path of madness and of war. The rest if they hold together are still strong enough not merely to resist their attack successfully—that is not what we want—but by clear warning to prevent that attack being made, and thus, by closing the road that leads to war, gradually to turn the aggressors towards the paths of peace. But this depends on two unsolved questions. Can the peace-lovers work with as much devotion and enthusiasm for truth and common sense as the war-mongers for what they call national honour, and we call falsehood and unreason? Can sober men stand up to fanatics? Or will the fury of a few madmen beat down the half-hearted resistance of many sane men?

And secondly, can nations that have been trained in an age-long tradition of cautious isolation, realize that the age for that has passed and that each one will perish unless all stand together? We have promised in the Covenant of the League to protect one another. For the first ten years that promise was kept, but of late, since the failure of the World Disarmament Conference in 1931–1933, the forces of peace have been progressively weakened, and on each occasion when a weak member of the League was attacked by an enemy, the strong members have looked on, mumbled a protest or an apology, and let the destroyer work his will. That is the road of old custom, of mental inertia, of the sluggishness that waits numbed and passive while all those who might befriend and help are destroyed one by one; the way of dead wood, not of the living tree.

Against this awful weight of blind tradition and bewildered selfishness let us throughout Europe who believe in Liberality and are free in thought

and speech see that our eyes are open and our
consciences alert; let us see that, under repeated
disappointments, our sane courage does not fail
us, till we or our children can at last, throughout
the world, bring to men of good will peace and
brotherhood.

cf. p# 26

Note on the Catechism —

"... to glorify God and enjoy him
forever ...."

" Consider the lilies of the
field and the birds of the
air ...."

" There was a lad with five loaves
and two small fishes ..."